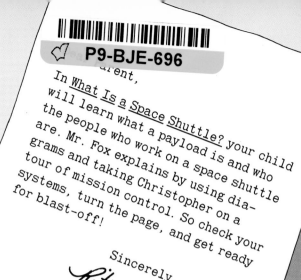

P9-BJE-696

...arent,

In <u>What Is a Space Shuttle?</u> your child will learn what a payload is and who the people who work on a space shuttle are. Mr. Fox explains by using diagrams and taking Christopher on a tour of mission control. So check your systems, turn the page, and get ready for blast-off!

Sincerely,

Rita D. Gould

Managing Editor

FAMILY FUN

- Take an imaginary voyage into outer space. Help your child design and draw a spacecraft. Then talk about things you would take with you, clothes you would wear, and things you would like to see and do in space.

- Make a space scene. Help your child draw, then cut out space shapes—planets, stars, comets, rockets, the moon— from construction paper or other heavy paper. Arrange the shapes on a flat surface and place a piece of drawing paper on top of them. Have your child gently rub over the drawing paper with a flat unwrapped crayon. A space scene will appear!

READ MORE ABOUT IT

- *Why Does It Fly?*
- *What Is Gravity?*

This book is a presentation of Weekly Reader
Books. Weekly Reader Books offers book
clubs for children from preschool through high
school. For further information write to:
WEEKLY READER BOOKS, 4343 Equity Drive,
Columbus, Ohio 43228

This edition is published by arrangement
with Checkerboard Press.

Weekly Reader is a federally registered trademark
of Field Publications.

WEEKLY READER BOOKS presents

What Is a Space Shuttle?

A **Just Ask**™ Book

by Chris Arvetis
and Carole Palmer

illustrated by
Vernon McKissack

FIELD PUBLICATIONS
MIDDLETOWN, CT.

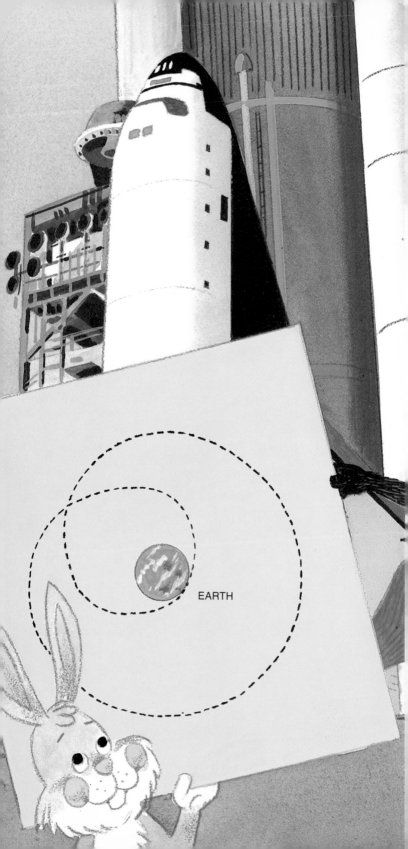

EARTH

First let's look
inside.
This part is the
flight deck.
It has computers
and thousands
of dials.

This part of the cabin
is the living area.
There is a place to fix food.
There is space to exercise
and wash up.
And there are bunks
to sleep on.

Another astronaut is a pilot.

The pilot is trained to fly the shuttle and is second in command.

The mission specialist is the head of the payload studies.

There may also be payload specialists on board. These people do not have to be astronauts, but they are trained to work with payloads.

They look busy!

People on the space shuttle have to learn a lot about space travel.

They practice everything that will happen on the trip in order to be ready to go into space.

ROCKET
BOOSTER

FUEL TANK

5-4-3-2-1-0 Blast off!
The power of the three
main engines and two
rocket boosters gets
the shuttle into space.
Once the shuttle is away,
the rocket boosters drop off.
The tank where the fuel was
stored drops off next.

There goes the
fuel tank into
the water!

As the shuttle travels through space, the payload specialists complete their tasks.

When the mission is finished,
the shuttle changes its course.
It turns and heads back to Earth.

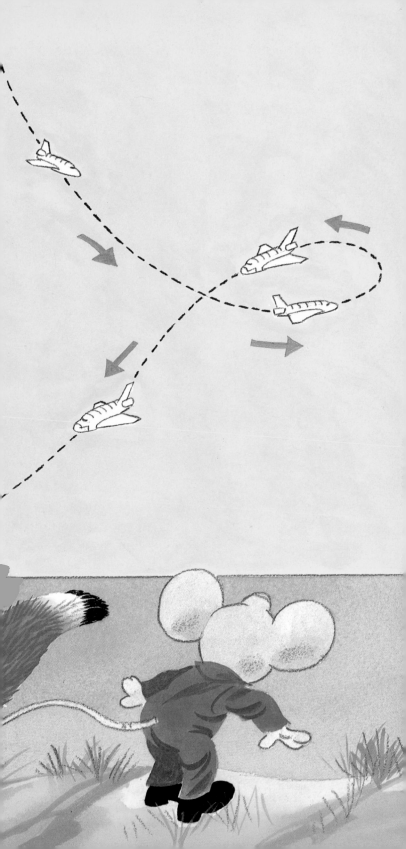

As the shuttle re-enters the earth's atmosphere, the shuttle glides in large S-curves back to Earth.

The ground crew checks the shuttle.

The astronauts are checked too.

The experiments go to the scientists to study.

Another space shuttle trip has made history.